I Am ... His~

I Am ... His~

This book is given to:

_____

I Am .. His~

On this ___ day of _____

In the year of _____

From: _____

I am

a Christian, a mother, a friend, a minister, a wife, a daughter, a sister, a politician, a teacher, a Gran-Gran, a poet, a principal, a volunteer, a business woman, a singer, a First Lady, a believer, an American, and

I am ...

HIS!

Written & Designed By:
Vivian L. Childs

V.L. Childs
Publishing

Warner Robins, GA 31095

CEO: Minister Vivian L. Childs
CFO: Dr. Henry Childs
COO: Henry Childs II, Esq.
D. O: Dr. Ashante Y. Everett
D. M: Nakeisha M. Curry, M.D.

Copyright © 2009 V.L. Childs Publishing

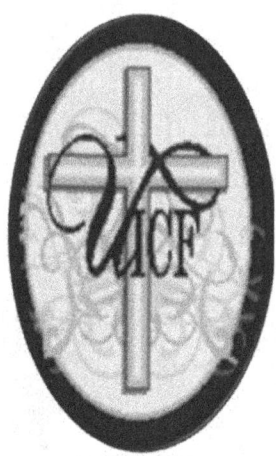

No part of this book may be reproduced, stored in a retrieval system, or transmitted by any means without the written permission of the publisher.

V.L. Childs Publishing
V.L.CHILDS/UICF LLC
P.O. Box 9334
Warner Robins, GA 31095
vlccreations@yahoo.com
www.vivianchilds.com

First published by V.L. Childs 2/13/2021
First created by Vivian L. Childs on 9/14/2013
ISBN 978-0-9799896-3-6

Author: Vivian L. Childs

Editorial Team: Dr. Henry Childs, Mack W. Curry III, Nakeisha M. Curry, M.D., Dr. Ashante Y. Everett

Cover/Layout design: Vivian L. Childs
All rights reserved.

Scriptures from the King James Version Bible

I Am ... His~

 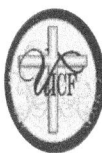

Table of Contents
Page Numbers

Introduction	6-9
Foreword	10-11
I am a Christian	12-15
I am a Mother	18-31
I am a Friend	34-37
I am a Minister	40-45
I am a Wife	48-57
I am a Daughter	61-63
I am a Sister	66-69
I am a Teacher	72-75
I am a Gran-Gran	78-88
I am a Believer	94-97
I am a Volunteer	100-103
I am a Business Woman	106-109
I am a Child of God	112-115
I am in the Political Arena	118-119
Sermon Epilogue	122-125
UICF/Bookings	126
Meet the Author	127
Your Inspirations	128-131
Acknowledgements	134
A Personal Journal for You	146-175

I Am ... His~

From the Kitchen of:
Vivian L. Childs, author of *I Am His* & *Splintered*

Recipe for: America

Add 50 states into a large bowl of diversity

Melt the diversity, then stir the sensitivity and the likeness into caring Americans

Evenly distribute faith, honor, and respect to restore a cohesive union of family

Roll laughter into the nation and allow it to rise to great heights

Individuals should be warmed in hope, not chilled by despair

Coat each idea, each thought, and each goal until fulfillment is reached

Agitation should be limited; never reaching a boiling point. Replace with love, then knead and handle with care.

A single person can make a change for America; but, many Americans, working together, can make significant changes that can and will benefit this country and all who live here.

Together we roll!   You decide~

I Am ... His is the epitome of who I am. God, in all of his wisdom and love, has showered His many blessings on my life. This book embodies my very being. I pray the contents within will strengthen and bless each & everyone who reads what is written.

I dedicate *I Am ... His* to my loving family & you.

Thank you to my husband, Henry, for giving me the wings to soar on the numerous journeys I have travelled. Admiration and endearment to my children, Nakeisha, Henry II, and Ashante, who I was blessed to birth and embrace on their incredible journeys to adulthood; to Demetris, a son I loved and who has departed to another location of holiness.

Much love to my extraordinary grandchildren, Mack (Trey), Alexis, Isabelle, Aralyn, Gordon (PAC), Alyssa, Victoria (Vicki), Shemetris, and Maddox.

A loving memory to my father, Isaiah Clark, better known as Chief; to my mother, Helen Clark, who is truly my best friend; my brother, Jerome Clark, who is one of the most brilliant men I know; and to my sister, Pamela C. Bohannon, who has a heart of gold (when she wants to) and impeccable nursing skills.

Lastly, to you, the reader:
"Look Up; Move Forward!"

I Am ... His~

How often are you given the opportunity to write your own story?

The purpose of this book is to afford you the opportunity to do just that.

After each section, pages are allotted for you to express your feelings. I have used stories, words of wisdom, and poetry to express to others who I am. You may do the same and then share who you are to others by passing this book to a special friend or loved one, or by simply using it as a journal for you.

Hence, *I Am ... His* is YOU!
I pray you will enjoy reading this book as much as I enjoyed writing it.

I Am ... His~

Whether a Christian, a mother, a dad, a husband, a friend, a minister, a wife, a son, a daughter, a sister, a teacher, a Gran-Gran, a poet, a Papa, a principal, a volunteer, a politician, a singer, a *First Lady*, a Pastor, a believer, an American, or *most importantly,* **HIS,**

YOU

can be one or several of the ABOVE~

Be Blessed!

FOREWORD

Let me tell you about Vivian Childs. First, there has never been a question of who she is or whose she is because she loves God and is content to operate in His way and in His timing. She is a relevant ripple through time whose influence is on-going. She has a treasure of experiences to share as seen through her strong Christian faith, love of God's people, and joy of living. To know Vicky is to know Ms. Helen, Vicky's mother. Ms. Helen is strong as she shows great love to her family, friends, and people she meets. She is also gracious. I saw her strength and graciousness as she said goodbye to her husband, Chief.

When Vicky laid eyes on Henry, I was there. Her decision to become Mrs. Henry Childs was decisive and instantaneous. Many people are mostly "just talk," but Vicky is a person of action. When Vicky met Henry, the family of Valbert and Mamie Walker was happy for Henry because if you know Henry, my cousin, you know he is not your run of the mill Black man. He has always been a piece of work, but we knew Vicky could handle *"it"* from jump.

I Am ... His~

FOREWORD

Because Vicky is a person of action, she remains hopeful. Vicky, we can't wait to see what God will prevail of your heart to share with us. Will it be about rearing your dynamic children or about the lives of the other children you have taught? Will we get to be a fly on the wall as you tell us about your military lives, here, there, and everywhere? Will we experience the flavor and places of your travels or will you instruct us on how to support a powerful man while maintaining your own identity and sanity. We can't wait.

Vicky, your book, *Splintered,* is good, and I plan to read it again. It is interesting, timely, and gives others a glimpse of your heart for God and His people. I can't wait to see who God is and what He will do in your life. Lastly, I want to thank you for allowing me to share your life and your love-light in this book, because I know that everybody is not strong enough to do even that. So, just know that it is my desire that you all continue to be blessed, and be a blessing.

Love, **Esther Denson**

I Am ... His~

I Am A Christian

What does it truly mean to be a Christian?

In this era of "if it feels good, do it," why would you or anyone else choose to be a Christian? Is it because it is fashionable? Is it because it's economical, or is it because you have been chosen to be a *Child of God*? If it is the latter, then do you really have a choice or do you simply need to claim your inheritance?

When I think about my life and the wonderful aspects of my being, I ask myself, who am I? Then I think of the most viable tool created for mankind, and I reach for it; the Bible.

Scripture says, *"I will praise thee; for I am fearfully and **wonderfully made**: marvelous are thy works; and that my soul knoweth right well.* Psalm 139:14-15.

What God has done is not just amazing, it's truly amazing!

I Am ... His~

I Am A Christian

I remember, as a girl growing up, singing the song "them bones, them bones, them dry bones" and singing how the thigh bone is connected to the leg bone, and the leg bone is connected to the ankle bone, and so on and so on. Every detail is precisely well orchestrated and designed, not a mere test model, to be efficient and made ready to wear.

My being a Christian, to me, dictates that I do some things; I am not ashamed to be different, I am not quick to anger, and even if someone does not know me by name, my actions will exemplify who I am.

I am a Christian is not to flaunt, or to judge, or to despise. This statement is to simply relate to others why I am a Christian, and maybe why you have chosen to follow the teaching of His Word and live life accordingly- as a Christian.

If I have to tell you I am a Christian, I truly believe my life is in contrast to what I believe. Prayerfully, my actions,

I Am ... His~

I Am A Christian

my words, and my walk is like a magnet for those things which are good, for those things which are holy, and for those things which are Christ-like.

I am a Christian and am proud to call His name; I am a Christian, and it's real, not a game.

Caring about and loving others, even when it is easier to hate, is a sacrifice I am willing to make on this journey. Are you?

Remember, He is who He is, and that's enough for me~

It Begins With Me

It begins with *me*
Life, liberty, and all that is free

It begins with *me*
The life I choose in this economy

It begins with *me*
Being sad or being happy

It begins with *me*
The values that are set for my family

It begins with *me*
Duty, honor, and responsibility

It begins with *me*

Integrity begins with *me*

Dignity begins with *me*
and most importantly,

being a Christian,
being a conservative,
and yes, voting my principles;

It all begins with me.

Inspirations from you~

Look up; move forward~

I Am ... His~

Inspirations from you~

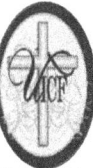

Look up; move forward~

I Am A Mother

Motherhood is a gift. More importantly, when it is done right, the stage of this development comes from a union where an egg is formed in the body and through an intricate process develops into a living being. A being, that is to be loved and at the right moment, is able and ready to instrumentally begin the process again. That, my friend, is motherhood.

Proverbs 23:25 Thy father and thy mother shall be glad, and she that bare thee shall rejoice.

I am a mother; yes I am. I remember what it took for me to be a mother. In the first few months of marriage, I was not trying to have a child because we were both still in school. But then, I started to wonder why it was not happening. Why was I not getting pregnant? I visited the doctor and was given all the medical advice I did not need, as well as different techniques to use, but to no avail. Finally, I decided I would try fertility pills. You notice I said, "I decided." I would get ahead of God's timing and bring on motherhood when I saw fit.

We have all heard that He will give you the desires of your heart; well, he did. When I went to the appointment to get the fertility pills, the doctor did a final test and lo and behold, my oldest daughter had settled in and would bless me on my first journey of motherhood.

What a beautiful expression of His love where through a union, an egg is formed in the womb and through this intricate process develops into a living being that is to be loved, to be cherished, and to be mothered.[19]

I Am A Mother

If I have achieved nothing else in my life, I feel like a gold-medal winner when it comes to being a mother. I love all of my children dearly; three I birthed, and many I simply claim and I love because I feel that they were sent to me, in order for me, to enrich their lives.

Don't think for one moment, that everything has always been peachy-keen. It has not. I was quite the disciplinarian; but, disciplined in and with love.

I remember the time when my teenager was one minute late coming through the front door and had not called for extended time out. I immediately woke my husband and said let's go. He thought I was out of my mind, but I knew something was wrong, and it was. Because I knew where my child was suppose to be, we traveled in that direction. Guess what, the car that my child and his friends were in had stopped. Remember, no cells phones back in the day. My husband was in total disbelief when our son made the comment to his friends, " I told you she was on her way." The trust that I have in my children and the trust they have in me as their mother shone brightly that night and still today.

Wow is the only word that comes to mind when thinking about the successes of our children with doctorates in Medicine, Law, and Education. Their successes overshadow known adversities that are sometimes expected in families of our makeup. To have careers of a physician (CMO of her own practice), an attorney (CEO of his own business), and an administrator (Elementary/Middle school Principal) is simply favor. By His grace, the branches of this favored tree continues to extend outwards to our grandchildren.

Thank you, Lord~

A Mother

According to Merriam-Webster, a mother is a female parent or woman in authority; *specifically*: the superior of a religious community of women. My mother is not defined by this definition; she is a definition for others to define.

When we think about mothers, we look at those women who have successfully raised children. My mother didn't just successfully raise children; my mother raised successful children and modeled how to raise successful children for others.

As a model of how to live an exemplary life, my mother reaches to her faith in *The Lord* to lead and guide her. She doesn't mimic His life; rather, He lives in hers. This allows her to be a sanctuary for others.

Many people try to manipulate illusions (our perception of them), instead of fixing their reality. My mother's reality is real and felt by people she meets. But why is she a great mother? My mother is my spiritual inspiration who shows me how to fight the good fight each day when the enemy is coming my way.

My mother is my inspirational leader who shows me how to keep going especially when I want to sit down. My mother was my reflection in the mirror when others looked at me and said this is not for you. My mother is my gift from God, my source of encouragement, my all and all, a great mother, the greatest mother.

Much love, Vivie
Ashante

My Mom is the GREATEST!

From My Son, Henry II

My mom is the greatest! That statement has become so common that it has lost some of its value. So, instead of proclaiming that I have the best mom in the world, I am going to prove it.

My mom is the greatest because of how she treats people. My mom treats people like they were made in God's image. She genuinely loves people for who they are, not for the status they hold.

My mom is the greatest because she sacrificed her life for others. I could list all of the things my mom has given up for her husband, her children, and her community, but the list would be too massive. I rather state how my mom's sacrifice has helped my family.

One of the ways you judge a mother is by her children. Based on that criteria my mom is a winner. She has three children: a doctor, a political advisor, and an educator. We all chose professions where just like our mom, we could help people. We all have continued my mom's tradition of sacrifice because we love her. Her voice is like medicine. It heals.

Although you could judge my mother by her children's success, I rather judge my mom by how my sisters and I feel about her. We love our mom. We love her so much; we call her almost every day. In fact, when she is unavailable to talk we get upset. We just want to talk to her.

I thank God for my mom everyday, and that's how I know my mom is the greatest!

Henry (H.C.)

From My Daughter, Nakeisha

D*ear reader,*

By now you have read my brother's and sister's wonderful accounts about how great, wonderful, and powerful our mother truly is. After reading their sections, I replied to my family, "Are you kidding me? I'm tapping out! I REFUSE to write anything after that!" I think they made mom do everything except walk on water!

Although I was completely serious and should have been respected (after all, I am the doctor in the family that everyone keeps mentioning), my decision was overruled (by my attorney brother) and I was verbally beaten (by my administrative sister). Therefore, I am writing my section. However, let me lay some ground rules:

1) This section will NOT be explaining how wonderful my mother is.

2) This section will NOT show you how she has conquered insurmountable obstacles and surpassed every given goal.

3) You will NOT need to restock your Kleenex during this section, because it will absolutely NOT overwhelm you with emotionally charged accolades that engage your heart and bring you to tears.

Why not, you ask? Because my over-achieving brother and sister have already done all of that in their sections. Therefore, rather than try to compete, out-write, and outwit them (because I can't), I will take the low road and scare you into loving her or make you scared not to.

For you see, although she stands only 5 feet tall (yes, mom...you are only 5 feet), the ground trembles under her every step. She's the princess you take to the ball, but once the clock strikes midnight, she's also the best friend you want behind you in the bar fight. She is loyal and will stand up for you (and with you) even when others have abandoned you and your cause. Because she is a God-fearing woman, you always have Christ in your corner.

She's the cleaner- not only the one who cleans your church, school, senior center, etc..., but also the one like the mob calls. You know... when you've made a mess, dug yourself into a hole, and can't see a way out. One call, and all of a sudden, judges change decisions, jobs appear, promotions occur, and second chances are granted. You never see her, but the

From My Daughter, Nakeisha

effects of her work are always present.

She's a comforter, but she's also the same woman who jumped across a table to confront a teacher who harassed my sister. Of course, she gracefully made everyone leave the room first, so there were no "eyewitnesses." However, the loudness in the room and the teach-teacher's psyche confirm the event. She holds people accountable for their actions and understands that intentions are nothing without integrity. She is honest and has an unwavering moral standard that guides her life.

Just great, right. Even though I promised not to brag about her, the words just keep coming out. She probably can't walk on water (because she is afraid of the ocean), but I would never dare her to. She just might try. In fact, God just might part the waters Himself; some might say that she has rescued people as Moses did. More often than not, people who meet her are enchanted by her. Her Godly spirit is contagious, and her service to others is unparalleled. I could never accurately portray how wonderful she is, so I'm glad I don't have to. God has truly blessed us with her, so I'll just tap out now (like I originally tried to do) and sum it up as I'm sure God will...

"Well done, good and faithful servant!"

P.S.
Mom... I love you more.

Nakeisha

Mrs. Childs

I Am A Mother-in-Law

"Her children stand and bless her." Proverbs 31:28.

Mrs. Childs, I think this is a verse that speaks to how important your role as a mother and mother-in-law has been. It reminds me how you have raised a truly blessed family, not only of your children but also those who have been fortunate to have you in their lives. You have been the cornerstone of the family and have set the example of how to live, worship, pray, and model the way. I have seen you set goals that seem impossible; however, at the end of the day there is not one goal that you have set that you have not achieved. This demonstrates your unrelenting drive and relentless pursuit to achieve your dreams.

G.E.

Now what does this all say to me?

Let me leave you with this thought. If children were to be adults, why would they need parents. Think about it. Just as I follow the rules set forth for me to abide by, children need then as well. Say what you mean and mean what you say. When older, children will thank you for having some restrictions and/or boundaries.

As a mother, I have a responsibility to train my children to be responsible adults.

Proverbs 22:6 Train up a child in the way he should go: and when he is old, he will not depart from it.

I also followed my parents teachings and loosened the rope, a bit, so my children could experience the world and all it holds. But, I held on tight enough so that when and if they needed to be reeled in, I was there, rope in hand, to help pull them through life's challenges.

That's Love! *~Vivian*

I Am ... His~

Inspirations from you~

Look up; move forward~

Inspirations from you~

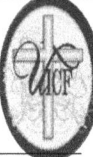

Look up; move forward~

VIVIAN CHILDS DEPICTS A VIRTUOUS WOMAN

Proverbs 31 illustrates the meaning of what characteristics you see in a virtuous woman; she shines as a bright beacon in this world of mass confusion, doubt, and hopelessness. She forecasts visions of precepts and warnings and portrays herself as an example of what needs to happen to change our circumstances.

Today, we see women of all ages following dubious role models, we are refreshed to find a timeless example of virtue, responsibility, and good sense. Here, in this lovely woman, is one who embodies the qualities which every believing woman should strive for in her personal life and appearance, in her family life, and in her daily duties.

I personally have seen her at the point of successfully making major conferences, political speakers, statesmen, and dignitaries feel the warmth of an event as if it was a comfortable living room environment. She possesses that gift that foresees the little details that can wipeout a major event if not handled correctly. Vivian, is a God sent woman for this time; throughout historical events, women have changed the outcome of wars, the hearts of Kings, and ceased the confusion of nations.

We need a leader of courage, kindliness, yet has a strong educational background with emphasis on strategies, community development, and civic involvement. What a complete package! She gets my vote, Georgia, Vivian Childs, is a winner!!!

Sincerely, **Yvonne Foreman**

A MOMENT OF SISTERHOOD

In our lifetime, we come across a lot of people for a reason, a season, or a lifetime. When I met Vivian L. Childs at a civic function, she came up to me and introduced herself. She made me feel comfortable as I was new to the organization hosting the event. Vivian and I did not communicate for almost a year until I found her information and

From A Friend

telephoned her regarding a question regarding the organization we were apart of. Well, out of that a sisterhood began to form, and years later we have a stronger relationship.

Vivian is a motivator, counselor, and confidant. She has a lot of the characteristics of an *"I AM"* Woman; she lives her life by example.

The icing on the cake was when Vivian and I discovered we shared the same birthday. How awesome to share your *born day* with such a phenomenal wife, mother, sister, aunt, cousin, friend, neighbor, teacher, and First Lady!

Vivian, wishing you continued success in all that you do!

Lelia Hagood (aka Missy)

UNDENIABLE LEADERSHIP

America needs leaders who are prepared to serve, but serve from a place of godliness and wholeness. America has found that in Vivian Childs. Vivian is a woman of conviction who is God-centered and focused on

I Am ... His~

From A Friend

building a nation that sustains us throughout the generations. A powerful speaker, leader, and motivator; she brings life to every task that she undertakes.

Vivian can organize and galvanize support in a way that brings results. With the heart of a lioness and the grace and compassion of a gentle southern lady, Vivian moves into action and provokes long-lasting, life-changing results. She balances life with such grace and possesses the many characteristics that are need-needed to move us into our future. A well-educated educator and writer, she is also a powerful speaker and is as comfortable speaking about her faith as she is about good government. She is a rare jewel who is as comfortable sitting and sharing with powerful generals as she is with the local guy who has lost his way and currently inhabits the local street corner.

I fully expect to continue to see great things of this dynamic woman on a local, state, and national level. Upward and Onward to the future with Vivian Childs!

Tonya Boga, Esquire

I Am ... His~

Inspirations from you~

Look up; move forward~

Inspirations from you~

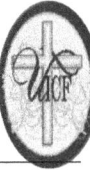

Look up; move forward~

I Am A Minister

Depending on who you talk to, women have no place in ministry; especially, if it is ministering to men. What joy I found, because I am a minister, when the following scripture answered the question concerning women in ministry, at least for me.

*Mark 1:31 And he came and took her by the hand, and lifted her up; and immediately the fever left her, and **she ministered** unto them.*

Did you notice the scripture said she, not he? The fever left *her*, and *she* ministered unto them.

The Real You is Inside of You! Powerful! I want you to know that you, alone with the guidance of God, and the words that He left for you, are sufficient because ***the real you is inside of you!***

When God grants you the gift of salvation, you invite Him to come into your life. In so doing, He equips you and enables you to accomplish great things. Why, because **the real you is inside of you!** He fills you with the Holy Spirit and uses you to make a difference. When God dwells in you, things that once were difficult, are now made easy in your life. He will use you to bring joy to others, He will use you to conquer the unthinkable, and He will use you to make a crooked path straight; because, **the real you is inside of you!**

Living in the cell phone and twitter generation, our lives are filled with things other than God. Let me tell you; your life and others around you are not enriched if you are not living for God, and that is why your downloaded ringtones are not always the songs that you think you ordered. Download JESUS and listen as He speaks to **the real you that is inside of you.**

I Am A Minister

We all know that we were not given a choice in how we were created; but, we can choose to live our lives according to His purpose. Remember, we are guided by the Holy Spirit and can accomplish the desires of our hearts because of that guidance.

On Sundays, many are given the opportunity to accept Jesus as their Lord and Savior. Yet, I have never seen long lines, or cheering, or folks pushing others down for this free opportunity. An opportunity to be fed by and filled with the Holy Spirit. However, I am reminded of all of the people waiting in lines, for hours, for a famous restaurant chain's Grilled Chicken. I mean for hours for food that was, "*free*." Do you know that people will camp out and even break down doors to receive free anything except salvation?

So, to those of us in ministry, what are we doing wrong? Well, I have an idea. I need somebody to tell everybody that there are churches offering free food every Sunday, seasoned by none other than the Master Chef. Better yet, tell them that when the doors of the churches open, they will not be given a rain-check and/or be asked to come back later. Guarantee them that they will be filled up on God's word and they won't need Dr. Anti-Gas and others for relief. Everything goes down easier with the Lord, and He chooses people like you and like me.

When you are chosen by God, you do not need a title, you do not need to be rich, and you do not need to be a celebrity, **because the real you is inside of you!** We are all great in the eyes of the Lord. He takes us just the way we are; no fancy resume is required.

I Am ... His~

I Am A Minister

Many times in our lives, we are broken, run over, and cut into small pieces by our decisions. We feel as though there is no hope. But no matter what has happened or what will happen, you will always find peace in Christ who loves you.

As I have often heard before, dirty or clean, bent over or straight, we are priceless to God. He loves us. The worth of our lives comes not in what we do, or who we know, but by who we are and most importantly, whose we are.

M omentary
I nfluence
N egates
I deology
S ubstance
T ruth
E xcellence
R elevance

I Am ... His~

PREACH

Preach, with passion

Preach, with style

Preach, with courage

Preach, with love

I Am A Minister

I Am ... His~

Inspirations from you~

Look up; move forward~

Inspirations from you~

Look up; move forward~

I Am ... His~

I Am A Wife

Nobody said it would be easy, but when it becomes difficult, put forth the effort to make it alright. After all, the vows do say, "for better or for worse. "Try loving instead of hating, and watch things change for the good of those concerned. ~*Vivian*

This photo moment reminds me of the song ***"Stand By Your Man."***

Live joyfully with the wife whom thou lovest all the days of the life of thy vanity, which he hath given thee under the sun, all the days of thy vanity: for that *is* thy portion in *this* life, and in thy labour which thou takest under the sun. **Ecclesiastes 9:9**

My Wife

I am honored to be a penman in this book. Where shall I begin, and if I begin, there is no ending. The *genesis* goes back to the University of Georgia on a day as if God opened up the skies and poured a street river as the rain fell. A rainbow, set in the sky, appeared to end on top of a beautiful seventeen-year-old young lady, shaped like a goddess with a large afro. I became awe- struck watching her sapphire eyes and her smile that sparkled diamonds. She appeared to be walking on the water, barefoot in the rain.

I knew from that moment on, as my heart palpitated, that spending the rest of my life convincing her to marry me would be my quest in life. I would learn that her name was Vivian Louise Clark. I can remember, that same day and at the hotel party that evening, how I played it cool and did not even ask her for a dance. Even during class registration, the next day in the University's coliseum, I found her amongst 18,000 people. I decided to trick her like I had done with the other young ladies. I would help her, since she was dressed in a mini skirt, get up on a three feet stage; It had worked

From My Husband

with other young ladies. She looked at me and said, "you would like that view from the bottom wouldn't you; I don't think so."

My relentless quest even drove me to sit in the University's Bulldog room and wait for her to get out of class, just to get a glimpse of her. I chased her for a year and a half, and we married on January 21, 1972, at the courthouse. I equate that day to the greatest day in my life. To my smiling amazement, I learned 35 years later, that at the hotel party, she told her roommate that I would be her boyfriend.

I elaborated on the beginning, because meeting Vivian was the beginning of my life. I have never met anyone like my wife. Each time I see her, I think of Genesis. God poured himself, full of love, compassion, miracles, and omnipotence into one person. I wake up each morning, starring at my wife as she sleeps, and begin my prayer with thank you Jesus for my wife. I can only describe her as a Vivian Wonder of the world. When God created her, he took an extra day, not seven but eight. As a life-enricher, she dedicates her life to helping others without asking anything in return. She makes the world better, leaving a piece of herself

I Am ... His~

through touching the lives of people in California, England, Georgia, Germany, Guam, Illinois, Japan, Kansas, Korea, Louisiana, Portugal, Philippines, Texas, and Venice. As she has touched your life, you may add your state to this list of states and countries.

My wife is the best friend to many. I have awakened at two o'clock in the morning, only to find my wife consoling someone on the telephone. She is a very present help in time of trouble. She is the most trustworthy person that I know. Her hallmark is integrity, love, and doing what is righteous. If you put a red light in the middle of the woods, my wife would stop at the red light. She is not a crowd pleaser, watcher, or follower. She is Vivian, a leader, innovator, and trailblazer. She has a radiant infectious smile that warms you from the inside out. A smile that makes you forget about your lingering problems and challenges. I accentuate her smile, because her smile springs forth hope in the lives of many people. You have to see it to believe it.

One day my wife went shopping and a lady, standing outside, looked distressed

From My Husband

my wife smiled and simply said, "how are you doing?" The lady said, "you don't really want to know." My wife informed the woman that she was a minister, and the lady poured her heart out to my wife. Afterward, the two parted company and went their separate ways.

After intensive shopping, as my wife departed the store, she heard a voice say, "there she is." To my wife's surprise, the policeman was talking to the lady whom my wife had previously consoled. The lady, talking loud, began to explain to the police that she was not shop-lifting. Her two friends, who rode to the store in her car, were being held in the police car for shoplifting. As the lady became more belligerent, the police handcuffed her and said you are going to jail. The lady said, "I can't go to jail because my daughter is with me." The man with her said, "I will take her home." However, the little girl snatched away and became upset and said, while crying, "I am not going with him." My wife smiled and began to talk to the little girl, and the little girl reached out and grabbed my wife's hand. The police in amazement, and out of normal protocol, simply said, "Ma'am you take her." The police gave the little girl to my wife; a lady that he nor the mom had known before. The Mom said, "please take care of her," and she gave my wife a telephone number to call. My wife took the little girl and her Mom's friend to a restaurant across the street, fed them, and delivered the little girl to her grandma once she arrived.

She is Holy Ghost filled, God fearing, and fervent in faith. While talking to a parent during my wife's 4th grade class field day, the parent's daughter remarked, "Mama don't you see Jesus in Mrs. Childs." The class called Mrs. Childs an angel; not their angel, but an angel. After taking the school's official 4th grade class photo, the students noticed that, it appeared, a halo was around Vivian's head. Hmmm.

My wife has an inner cross on her forehead that is visible to many, especially to those that have a void in their life. While in a craft store, a little girl, about seven years old, ran up to my wife and began a conversation. They discussed cooking, dolls, and tea sets. As the conversation progressed, the girl wanted to take my wife home with her. She became emphatic and loud with anticipated joy, asking her mom if my wife could come home and play at their house. The mom tells the little girl that the lady (my wife) "do not know them." The little girl gets even louder and says she is my friend. To my amazement, this was the first time my wife had ever laid eyes on the little girl.

All that I am and will be is because of God and my wife. God created me, and Vivian developed me. Passing by a recruiting station, my wife remarked you need a job, why don't you go in and take the Armed Forces Aptitude Test to become a pilot. To make her happy, I scheduled the test, knowing I would be accepted into Law School long before the results came back. As fate would have it, I passed the test with flying colors and got accepted into the Navy to become a pilot and into the Air Force to become a Navigator. Fresh out of college, married, and bills piling up, I took the first job offer available, the Air Force. My wife not only willed me in the Air Force, but she had a vision of my assigned aircraft and first assignment. One day, she saw a large camouflaged, black and green aircraft flying in the pattern. She rushed home to tell me that I would get that aircraft out of navigation school. I thought, "she is wrong this time." The Air Force assignment team had stated that no more B-52 assignments would be given out to crewmembers. A month later, she dreamed that we were on an island with one of her friends from high school. I thought she was losing her mind. I guess I was the only one astonished when the assignments came down, and I was assigned to this black and green B-52 on the Island of Guam. My wife simply said, "I knew a long time ago where we were going."

What shall I say to all these things? People love her after talking to her for one minute. She knows and has visions of things before they occur, she is said to be a mother to all, and she finds joy in solving others' problems. She labors through physical pain, but heals others' pain. With astounding perseverance, resilience, and the wisdom of Solomon, she bears her cross and picks up the cross of others without saying a murmuring word. What shall I say to all these things? Simply, this is my beloved *Wife*, in whom God and I are well pleased.

I Am A Wife

Again, nobody said it would be easy, but the joy of marriage and all that it embodies is well worth any negative hiccups of life; that is, when you are yoked with *your* life partner; not an infatuation. *~Vivian*

The Word, says, *"Whoso findeth a wife findeth a good thing and obtaineth favour of the LORD."* **Proverbs 18:22**

Excerpts From Proverbs 31

*W*ho can find a virtuous woman? for her price is far above rubies. [11] The heart of her husband doth safely trust in her, so that he shall have no need of spoil. [12] She will do him good and not evil all the days of her life. [5] She riseth also while it is yet night, and giveth meat to her household, and a portion to her maidens. [20] She stretcheth out her hand to the poor; yea, she reacheth forth her hands to the needy [23] Her husband is known in the gates, when he sitteth among the elders of the land. [25] Strength and honour are her clothing; and she shall rejoice in time to come. [26] She openeth her mouth with wisdom; and in her tongue is the law of kindness. [27] She looketh well to the ways of her household, and eateth not the bread of idleness. [28] Her children arise up, and call her blessed; her husband also, and he praiseth her.

If you are married, or not married, do you, as I, find these verses to be thought provoking? So many find marriage to be minuscule and not like a piece of fine silver that through the years often times tarnish. Comparably, with a little love and some gentle polishing, perks back up and becomes the piece you were initially drawn to love and admire. What am I saying? I am saying, "make sure what you want is what *He* wants for you. There is a difference.

~*Vivian*

I Am ... His~

Inspirations from you~

Look up; move forward~

Inspirations from you~

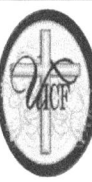

Look up; move forward~

WHY MOTHERS ?

W hen ever the going gets tough,
H e provides us what we need
Y ou and I are blessed, because,
she carries the seed.

M others shape and mold ,
O ften keeping watch as we lay;
T eaching, leading, and guiding along the way.
H elping at any cost, each and every day
E xcepting life's challenges with grace and love.
R eaping God's blessings as graceful as a dove,
S owing the seeds that are showered from above

Is why He gave us Mothers to love.

My Daughter

My daughter, Vivian, is one of the best daughters anyone can have. It took my husband, Isaiah, and I five years from the birth of our first child to have Vivian, and when she was born, we knew God had sent us an *angel*. She came here differently, and she is still different today.

Vicky is the drum major of her own band; she keeps in step with the Lord, not man. When she is your friend, you have a friend indeed. She does not care about your status in life, your status in politics, or how much money you have in the bank. She treats everybody the same. Our family has been blessed to see Vicky's heart through her caring, day to day living. You are blessed to see Vicky's heart through the stroke of a computer key. To know her is to love her; we do."

Vicky is kind, sweet, loving, and a helping hand. She loves people, does great things for people, and is always willing to take care of others. I couldn't ask for a better daughter than Vicky or share a better person with others. She

From My Mom

readily gives advice, great advice, and is always there to take children under her arms. Vicky (most of her family calls her Vicky, but you know her as Vivian), your mother, Mrs. Helen Clark, will always love you and is proud that you have written another book that will help others through love and inspiration for one another.

Your mom, *Helen Clark*

> *Ezekiel 13:17* Likewise, thou son of man, set thy face against the **daughter**s of thy people, which prophesy out of their own heart; and prophesy thou against them,
>
> But Jesus turned him about, and when he saw her, he said, Daughter, be of good comfort; thy faith hath made thee whole. And the woman was made whole from that hour. *Matthew 9:22*

I Am ... His~

Psalm 127:3-4

I Am A Daughter

*"Fear not, for I am with you;
Be not dismayed, for I am your God.
I will strengthen you, Yes, I will help you,
I will uphold you with my righteous right hand."*

Isaiah 40:10

Lo, children are an heritage of the LORD: and the fruit of the womb is his reward.

I Am ... His~

Inspirations from you~

Look up; move forward~

I Am ... His~

Inspirations from you~

Look up; move forward~

I Am ... His~

I Am A Sister

Mark 3:35 For whosoever shall do the will of God, the same is my brother, and my **sister**, and mother.

Proverbs 18:24 A man that hath friends must shew himself friendly: and there is a friend that sticketh closer than a brother.

A Brother and His Sister

I have known Vivian all of her life and watched her develop traits and character that I see manifested in her today in both the political and religious arenas.

Of all of her accomplishments and accolades, the things that keep her grounded and humble are the lessons she learned from her parents: quick thinking from her mother and self-worth, patience, and fearlessness from her father. Her father, Isaiah, was God-fearing, a gentle spirit, and had a smile that could melt a glacier.

The most important thing that Vivian learned and where there is no compromise is the love and importance of family. If you are unfortunate to tread in the aforementioned territory, beware and be prepared to meet, "Louise."

Love you, Sis
Jerome Clark

Sister To Sister

My one sister, Vicky, is my only sister. I love her, and she is totally different from me. She's smart and she's out starting things. She is smarter than me on some things and not smarter than me at others. For instance, I am far more streetwise, and she is more connected politically. The things that I would do, she would not do, and the things she does, I won't do; meaning, we are totally opposite. Again, I am more streetwise, and she is more educated, sophisticated-wise; but, we love each other, and we always have each other's back. Even though we are opposite, there is nothing we will not do for each other or with each other.

As sisters that are totally opposite, we are very much connected and indebted to each other. No matter how many miles separated us, if anything came up and I needed her, she was always there for me.

Growing up, I wanted to hang around her a little bit too much sometimes. She would leave and go out, and my brother would always bring me where she was. What is funny is my brother would leave before the party or outing was over, and Vicky would have to bring me home; loved it.

I love you, sis, always and forever~

Your only sister,

Pamela C Bohannon

From My Sister

I Am ... His~

Inspirations from you~

Look up; move forward~

Inspirations from you~

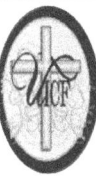

Look up; move forward~

I Am A Teacher

One of the highlights of my being is being called mom by several of my students as well as by several of my children's friends; not because they were not being loved by their own mom, but I am told because of the motherly love I showered on them.

> **Proverbs 22:6**
> Train up a child in the way he should go: and when he is old, he will not depart from it.

It has been stated that I have served the community as an education ambassador and as an education champion. In accordance, I was blessed to implement the Odyssey of the Mind program at my school. After having teams to win at the regional and state levels within two years of the program, I, along with wonderful coaches and parents, took a team to the World Finals in Iowa. They were blessed to participate in a competition that included teams from Poland, Japan, Singapore, and other counties and United States cities.

Upon discovering a substantial adult illiteracy rate in this community, the Learning with Love program was founded and set the course for adults who would otherwise not attempt to pursue their GED.

Working with a local technical college, the LWL program achieved what others deemed impossible. Individuals were mentored to see themselves not as they were, but as they could be, as they were guided through the college's registration process.

While others considered their efforts a success, our team realized that success is achieved through graduation. As a result, we coordinated transportation, set up performance and progress assessments for each student, provided a tutoring service, and set up a reward recognition program. Consequently, our efforts were praised, and we celebrated when our efforts resulted in seeing a student obtain a *GED*.

Learning with Love has not only improved individuals self-worth and confidence, but has also created the opportunity for individuals to become a more valued individual in the community. Using a local church as a launching platform, our efforts led to my being invited to serve on the Houston County Certified Literate Community Program. The CLCP was in partnership with the local college serving our program.

From a Parent Who Became a Trusted Friend

Vivian Childs was my son's, Tyree, 4th grade teacher. When I left him at school, I knew he was in the care of someone who loved him as much as I did. Vivian was his second momma that year. When he struggled in spelling, and it was taking a toll on his self-esteem, she immediately called a parent/teacher meeting. She explained how hard he was being on himself, and she had a plan of action she was going to put in place for him; not only to excel in spelling, but to help him rebuild the confidence she saw he had lost. Vivian incorporated God in every subject she taught Tyree; his spiritual growth was a big concern to her as well.

I struggled that year with, "was I doing right by my son?" I was a young Christian, not raised in a Christian home. Vivian gave me practical tools, and spiritual tools to use with my son. Vivian also gave me encouragement when I need-needed it. She took so much time out of her busy day to sit and listen to my fears and concerns with wisdom that comes from being a mature Christian, and momma, who had walked

I Am ... His~

From A Parent

my shoes with her own children and grandchildren.

I have long admired Vivian, and no matter how many days go between our talking, we always pick up where we left off. Vivian always starts by catching up on Tyree and the latest "going ons" in his life.

Vivian has invested so much of herself in me, without probably knowing she was making a difference. She was just living out the Christian life that attracts so many to her. Vivian is one of those rare and precious friends that I am so thankful God put in my path. **His** loving hands made it possible for our paths to cross so many years ago. I love you, Vivian.

AnnJeanette Baptiste

And God hath set some in the church, first apostles, secondarily prophets, thirdly *teachers*, after that miracles, then gifts of healings, helps, governments, diversities of tongues.

1 Corinthians 12:27-29

I Am ... His~

Inspirations from you~

Look up; move forward~

Inspirations from you~

I Am A Grandma/Gran-Gran

What will I leave thee?
Do you have a legacy?

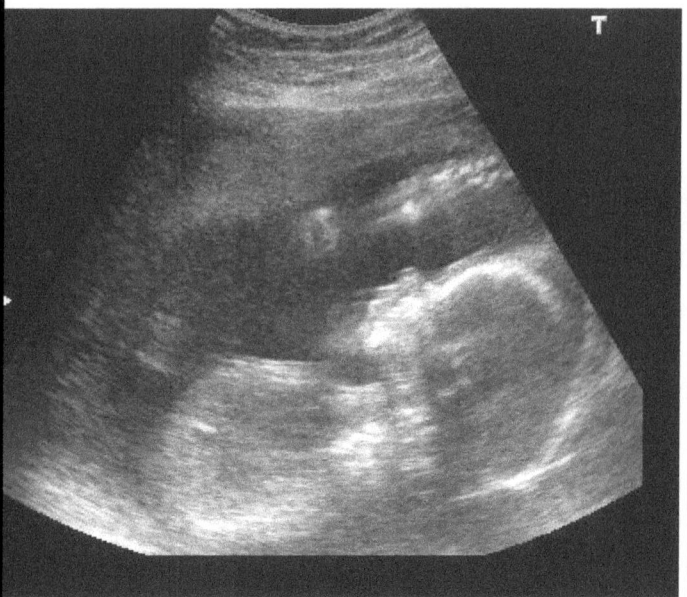

Every time I see this ultrasound picture of my grandchild, I marvel at **His** wondrous works. Safe, secure, waiting patiently, not needing anything. Every moment of development depending on the care given by his mother, my lovely daughter.

I ask myself, "how in the world have I been so blessed, so favored, and so proud to be called a grandma by some and a Gran-Gran by others?"

My Grandmother

Grand is correct as told by my uncle, her son. A warm and powerful mother as proclaimed by my aunt, her daughter. A marvelous combination of both as true and as blue as the sea as reasoned by my mother, her daughter. What more can be said or done? What more could I alone say to lift such a marvelous woman higher than her own children have already done? What more could I do to show the world that she is nature's greatest mystery, yet one of the Lord's greatest gifts to mankind. She touches people she has never met in ways they will never know. She teaches people who cannot learn to grow wiser. This growth should be less from their experiences and more from those around them. A gift, a boon, a solace in the darkness, she is light unparalleled, she is a force unstoppable, she is a mind all-knowing, she is a sparkle glaring...*She Is My, Grandma.*

Dusk approaches my dearest readers... The sun is setting, its warmth leaving the cool grasp of the world. The moon has risen to dance in the night sky twirling the stars about its waist, calling the sea to meet its gaze. I invoke

From My Grandson, Mack III

the Muse, which gave the poet Homer the words he needed to complete the Odyssey. I pray that the Lord grant me the presence of the angel Gabriel that I might compose a piece worthy of my grandmother's ethereal presence.

I ask thee all, channel your thoughts into one location. View the mind as a pallet in which I shall paint the image of a woman so beautiful, so marvelous, so transcendent, that time itself seems to slow down so that it can watch her live longer, that space bends and weaves so that it does not hinder her journey to greatness. Your thoughts are in one spot, your mind is clear, you are ready for the stroke of my brush; listen, as I tell you of the greatest person of our time.

Walk through the valleys of the shadow of death, defeat the darkness which claws the soul with nails as chilling as a blizzard, as sharp as a blade. Dive into the depths of the abyss known as the Mariana Trench and feel the crushing pressure surround the body as if it were your own skin. Climb higher than the tower of Babel and gasp for breaths of air as the altitude almost seems to take it all away. Trek through the Sahara desert with its blistering winds, scorching heat, and seemingly endless terrain of sand and stone. Survive these mortalities, and you shall gain insight into what empowers a woman such as this. Death is not an enemy to her nor those around her as she lifts them high above its tentacles and shows that it is not a part of life, but an end to a journey. She's an end to the toil and labor of troubles and problems, mischief and sins, despair and solemn. She is a way back home. She can show you that a life lived to its fullest is not necessarily a good life. She can show you that a life lived for the glory of God far surpasses the glamorous life of a movie star facing the packs of critics and heretics. Though the ocean she does not wish to surmount, she is a testament of how little fear can stop ambition. As I can recall her on a beach, crossing a mile of sand, she found the resolve to wade in what many would believe to be her greatest enemy. She took on the waves and did not falter to her instinct to panic, yet took in what her senses gave her. Water no longer had its power over her; she had power over water. Planes do not suit her desires as well, but does this stop her from achieving her goals? I can recall another time where she bit her distaste and climbed on a plane to see her

I Am ... His~

From My Grandson, Mack III

her grandchildren, my sister and me. Thousands of miles into the air yet she faced it down without care for she had a goal, a purpose, a desire to reach her destination and accomplish her wish.

Some intrepid people call life a tenuous desert. Some craven people call it a demon which draws on the lives of all who dare oppose it. Life is bountiful for such a woman as genuine as this. If she was a plant, she would be a beautiful cherry blossom tree which bestows splendor to the scenery in which it is present. Youthful with life as abundant as the blossoms that fall in the autumn breeze. As magical as the colors it presents in the harshest of winters.

If I could write an epic poem so powerful that it could quake the earth, split mountains, stop the wind, extinguish the sun, and parch the ocean… maybe then could I describe a woman as lovely as she. Maybe then I could find the strength, ability, acuity to capture all her great works, all her daring deeds, all her cherub expressions into one piece of literature which could captivate the world. Maybe then could I tell you that the answer to true peace, is this majestic woman I can call with pride, my grandma.   p.s. I love you the most,

Shadow Vanguard

Abyss of Shadows (Mack Curry III) ***Trey***

I Am ... His~

Me and My Grandma

My grandma means so much to me. Her smile lights up the whole room. Me and my grandma are really close, and she is always there for me. She is always thinking of others before herself. Me and my grandma always go shopping together when I come to visit. She has really good taste, and we always find something cute to wear. I love her warm hugs, and her delicious home-cooked meals.

My grandmother, Vivian Childs, is a wonderful, intelligent, and determined woman. She is a great person to talk to and is a great listener. She is very motivated and motivates others. She is a down to earth type of woman and is just a great person altogether.

Love You, Grandma,

Alexis S. Childs,
Author of
Sky Phoenix

Sky Phoenix

Written and Illustrated by: Alexis Samara Childs

From My Granddaughter, Alexis

I Am ... His~

Grandma

*G*ran-Gran, I think you are the kindest, most sweetest person there is. You are the *light* in the dark, the *flame* to the candle. You are one of the best things that has ever happened to me. I love you so much; words cannot even explain my love for you. I do hope that one day, I will turn out like you. You are perfect to me. You make mistakes, but then fix them and they always change my life.

You are my other mother and know all there is to know. You are there when I need you, and you take care of me. Again, you are the nicest person I know, and I love you for that. I can always count on you to be there for me and listen to what I have to say. You are also a good problem solver and know the correct answer to most questions. People can always count on you to be there for them and for me.

One day I will follow in your footsteps. It may not be today or tomorrow, but one day. I could not ask for a better grandma (Gran- Gran) than you, Mrs. Vivian L. Childs. I will always love you from the bottom of my heart. **I will always, always love you!**

From My Granddaughter, Aralyn

Aralyn Y. Everett

My Super Hero

I am *Alyssa Curry,* and I have an amazing grandmother. You see, she is not like other grandmothers whom you love just because they bring you presents. No, not my grandmother. She is a *superhero* to me. When someone is sad or if anybody needs anything, she has the power and the courage to save the day. My grandmother is the best person to give you hope, love, and trust. My grandmother is the best thing that ever happened to me. I am so glad that she is a part of me, because that makes me a *superhero* too.

This is a picture of me and my amazing grandma. She makes me feel like the sun is always shining on me. Flowers bloom all around her, and her love fills the air. She is super smart and sweet and will melt your heart. I love her soooo much!

Alyssa

I Am ... His~

From My Grandchildren, Gordon

Gran-Gran

Being Vivian Childs' grandson is a very extraordinary experience. There is never a time when my grandmother is sitting down and doing nothing. She is always trying to do something for other people. She always is trying to make my life better.

My grandmother is loving, caring, patient, and most of all she is an American.

I wish I could see her more often.

PAC (Gordon Everett II)

GRANDMA

You are one of the best Grandmas in the world. You make me smile. Your eyes brighten the sun.

Love,

Maddox Childs

My Grandma

Grandma is worth more than all the money in the universe. I love the sweet sound of her voice and how her laugh wakes up the room. Grandma means the world to me, and I bet I mean the world to her too. She is one of my best friends.

Love,
Isabelle Childs

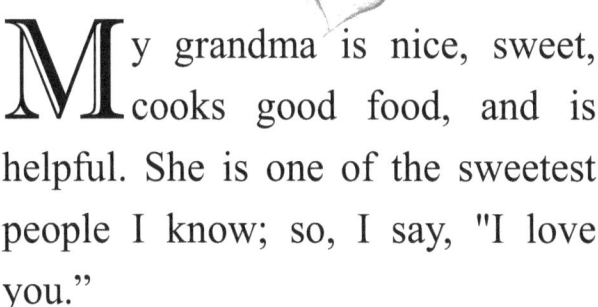

My grandma is nice, sweet, cooks good food, and is helpful. She is one of the sweetest people I know; so, I say, "I love you."

Arnetta Childs

I Am ... His~

From My Granddaughter, Victoria

She's My Grandma

Y ou make the sun shine. You are the best. Thank you for being my grandma. You mean a lot to me.

Love,

Vicki (Victoria Childs)

I Am ... His~

My Doll, Since the Age of Three Years, Penny

At the age of three, I received a life-size three-year-old doll for Christmas. Penny has travelled the world, with me and my family, and is a conversation piece amongst the grandchildren. In fact, excitedly, one of my grandchildren asked, "grandma, do you know that Penny can not talk?" ***Enough said~***

I Am ... His~

In Memory! 15 Years with CoShep

Mother's Day, 1984, I received an *unasked-for* surprise. The surprise would later be called CoShep, a German Shepherd/Collie mix who looked more like a German Shepherd than like a collie.

CoShep became a part of our lives and at times amazed others with his behavior. He did not have the tendencies of jumping up on or having to sniff people when they entered our home. So blessed to have such a wonder for so many years!

A Commentary Reflecting Children

We, grown-ups, ruin children's beautiful minds by telling children that a sky should be colored blue, that people can only have two eyes, or that unicorns don't really exist. Each redirection/correction sequentially destroys creative synapses and leads our children down a road of normality and mediocrity. For this reason, I have encouraged our children and our grandchildren to embrace their creativity.

Because children's minds have not been re-trained, they are able to tap into parts of their imagination that are lost to many of their peers When joining them on their journey to adulthood, I invite you to remove all of your preconceived notions of *normal*. Just for a moment, embrace the pure, illogical regions of your mind that *once* made everything possible with only a blink of an eye.

Remember:
We, too, once were children ~ VLC

Inspirations from you~

Look up; move forward~

Inspirations from you~

Look up; move forward~

I Am A Believer

We need to stop the fussing, and the fighting, and reap the joys of life. Seriously, enough is enough. Look how close we are to danger. Lives gone in a twinkling of an eye. Doesn't the Word speak of it? You may not have tomorrow to say I am sorry, or I made a mistake. I tell youth this all of the time... enough is enough.

Are you aware that when God puts a stumbling block in front of you, it is for a reason? Ask yourself this question. "Why have you been saved?" Understand, this question is for everyone; babies, tots, teens, young adults, millennials, seniors, and everyone includes me. You know what's funny? I woke up one morning and wrote what I thought was going to be the Word for a Sunday service. I still believe it was a good Word for that day; but for a strange reason, I misplaced what I had written and had to rely on Him to replace that particular sermon with a different one. My question again, "Why have we been saved?" Have you thought about the question? I once heard that we have been saved not .

merely to avoid evil, but to do good. Therefore, the people of Christ should not be known primarily for what they don't do, but for what they do.

You recall how Paul said it in Ephesians 2:10, "*We are God's workmanship, created in Christ Jesus for good works, which God prepared beforehand, that we should walk in them.*" And you recall how he said it in Titus 2:14, "*[Christ] gave himself for us to redeem us from all lawlessness and to purify for himself a people for his own possession who are zealous for good works.*" and then (I will continue to quote scripture), do you remember the words of Jesus, "*Let your light shine before others, so that they may see your **good works** and give glory to your **Father** who is in heaven.*" Here's another one: "*Whatever you do, in word or deed, do everything in the name of the Lord Jesus, giving thanks to God the Father through him.*" Love this one, *He was wounded for our transgressions; he was crushed for our iniquities; upon him was the chastisement that brought us peace, and with His stripes we are healed.*

Christ lived perfectly, not only to become our righteousness, but also to show us how to live.[95]

I Am ... His~

Inspirations from you~

Look up; move forward~

Inspirations from you~

How are we doing? Are we at least trying? Are we succeeding? Do we care? Does it matter to anyone? If it does, then as we invite Christ in, we should be ushering the enemy out. The enemy will never win unless we allow the enemy in our lives. So, when Christ arrives, "The Spirit of the Lord will be upon us."

No one knows the time, the hour, the place, or the circumstances that will cause us to leave this place. Some may remember the sermon that I preached, "Can you answer the call?" That question is not a joke to me; it is for real. I am not quite sure how it will be, but what will be your answer when He asks you, "why didn't you do some things you could have done?" What will you say when He asks, "why didn't you feed your brother when your brother was hungry, or why didn't you clothe your sister, when your sister didn't have a blouse to put on, or why didn't you drive someone when all they had were their feet to get them from place to place, or why you said no when your answer could have and should have been yes?"

Why do we bicker, when we should be rejoicing and why are we looking down when all of our help, and all of our strength, and all of the desires of our hearts come from the Lord. The pages of this book are open, and if you feel led to invite Him into your heart, today is your day to say, **" I surrender all."**

> ***Psalms 139:13-16*** *For thou hast possessed my reins: thou hast covered me in my mother's womb. I will praise thee; for I am fearfully and wonderfully made: marvellous are thy works; and that my soul knoweth right well. My substance was not hid from thee, when I was made in secret, and curiously wrought in the lowest parts of the earth. Thine eyes did see my substance, yet being unperfect; and in thy book all my members were written, which in continuance were fashioned, when as yet there was none of them.*
>
> .***Ephesians 2:10*** *For we are his workmanship, created in Christ Jesus unto good works, which God hath before ordained that we should walk in them.*

I Am A Volunteer

This chapter was difficult for me to write as I felt like I might be tooting my own horn, and that is simply not who I am. So, I enlisted the services of my husband, and he wrote this segment for me and about me.

Vivian's leadership touches all aspects of Warner Robins and the State of Georgia. She sits on several boards to include chairing the Gordon College/Museum of Aviation GYSTC (Georgia Youth Science Technology Center. GYSTC is a dynamic and highly successful organization that is engaged in addressing both the national and the Georgia crises in science, math, engineering and technology (STEM) education through quality programs for certified teachers, students, and their parents.

GYSTC provides teachers with training, innovative curriculum and hands-on activities that enable students to learn and understand through doing, and to involve families in supporting that learning.

Vivian epitomizes service before self. From serving on committees to serving on the Feed the City's food and cheerleading lines, Vivian makes the community in which she lives, a valued community. She was personally called on to use her experience to give life to an organization in need of assistance.

I Am ... His~

In her well doing, she never complains. Vivian used her experience as an educator to develop a strategic plan and organized volunteers to provide mentoring, tutoring, and programs for youth. Vivian has been a solid foundation whose efforts have improved youth programs and has helped youth to cope with complex issues and scenarios that are brought on by peers and difficult social environments; she was trained as a peer counselor. Whether it is taking kids out to entertainment parks, to cultural enlightenment events, or to functions to reinforce social behavior, Vivian creates hope and builds self-esteem. Her efforts have achieved remarkable results. Vivian's mentees see school from a different perspective which has accounted for an improvement in grades and school behavior.

When a local association needed resuscitation, Vivian took over the Presidency and led the organization. She developed a strategic path that invigorated private enterprise, government, and community involvement and support. As a result, the non-profit organization set a new course in generating revenue, providing cultural events, and enhancing the community.

Realizing the value of art culture, Vivian and a local art association partnered with schools to establish the Meet the Master program. Renowned local artists, visiting schools to share their knowledge and talents with students, served as an inspiration for higher intellectual achievement and art to achieve the dreams of the children in the program. As a result, student displays were featured at a local event.

Vivian also wrote a grant to help orchestrate an Art Extravaganza to provide cultural enrichment for the community. Vivian, and others in the Alliance, tremendous efforts put together an all-star team comprising of Macon State College, Houston County Schools, local churches, performing art groups, artists, and the business community. As a result, this event raised awareness and stimulated innovation.

Vivian is highly involved in the community. She has served on the Chamber of Commerce's Board of Directors, Educational Affairs, Military Affairs & Government Affairs committees; sat on a School Board, and served as chairman of the County Board of Elections.

She serves on CGTC's Adult Education Advisory Board; has chaired several other boards, committees, and partners with local agencies on community projects: Annual Back to School Bash sponsor, International City Fall Festival, Habitat for Humanity, and Community Outreach Thanksgiving initiatives, to name a few.

Vivian is currently the First Lady of her church and the youth minister. Her former involvement includes: served on a Diversity task force, trained as a Peer-counselor, and served as a Wedding and Event coordinator. She implemented the Odyssey of the Mind Program and orchestrated State Senatorial and Congressional visits at her school.

Vivian has the distinction of receiving a " key to the city" from two different mayors, being recognized during Women History and Black History Month activities, being a keynote speaker for women retreats, and being recognized as a Middle Georgia's finest by the "I Think I Am Foundation."

Vivian has become known as Mom, mentor, and confidant. Vivian plans, organizes events, and raises the funds to provide enriched activities. These functions serve to provide youth an environment to foster and nurture in becoming society leaders. Her ministry reaches worldwide through her website. She is passionate about her work in the ministry and is sought out to speak and sing at various events. She sang the National Anthem at a Veterans event in front of a City Hall, and other political, social, retirement, and fundraising events. A Judge invited her to sing the National Anthem at his installation ceremony.

I Am ... His~

Speaker Request Form for Vivian L. Childs

Event Name -

Event Date -   Event Start & End Time -

Event Location -

Address -   City/State/Zip -

Location Phone -   County -

Purpose of the Event -

Event Contact -   Position/Title -

Phone (Office) -   Cell -

Mailing Address -
City -   State -   Zip -

Email -
Media Relations Contact - Phone -   (Cell)

The Role of Speaker at the Event:

___ Featured Speaker/Keynote   ___ Brief Remarks/
___ Greetings ___ Recognized Guest ___ Panelist/Honoree

Meet the Author

Vivian L. Childs, CEO & Founder of VLChilds/UICF LLC, is the published author of **"Splintered,"** *Brokenness in the Political Arena.* **Are We Sacrificing America for Political Gain?** The book is a collection of the ins and outs of politics, patriotism, and faith. It is a collection of thoughts and experiences from a vast array of everyday people who just want to make America better. As Childs has exemplified through her years of political activism and volunteerism, it is not hard to understand why she chronicled these stories.

Vivian is a former Congressional Candidate and Congressional District Chairman. She left teaching to become the visionary of her business. As a visionary, who is eager to see the community improve their quality of life, Vivian brings passion and energy to serving those in her local community and is noted for performing random acts of kindness. She hosted the "It's Time" Unity Conference which honored and presented prestigious awards to outstanding women in different career fields.

Vivian, as a Delegate Surrogate at a National Convention, delivered the first motion from the floor. She spoke at the National Women Political Caucus, and the Palladian View Women's Summit. She is the event .host for an annual 9/11 ceremony.

I Am ... His~

Inspirations from you~

Look up; move forward~

Inspirations from you~

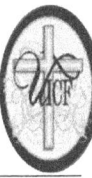

I Am ... His~

I Am A Business Woman

Through my business, VLCHILDS/UICF, LLC, I have done publishing, tutoring, men-mentoring, and GED prep. I had been involved in youth ministries and over the past years have changed my focus to women ministries. I am focused on developing women to be of the greatest potential that they are designed to be.

As founder and Executive Director of UICF, I provide services to enhance the community through volunteerism and academic empowerment. Additionally, the "It's Time" Unity Conference joins other states and communities that honor and recognize women. As we all know, in America, women come from different places and backgrounds; however, despite their differences, they all share a common thread. The thread they share is their unique ability to support and serve their local communities.

UICF's goal is to host the Unity Conference each year, the first Saturday in March, to recognize women in different career fields. It all began in 2010 when *First Ladies* were honored. Since that time,

Women in Education, Women in the Armed Forces, Women in Business, Women in the Medical Field, and Power Women have been honored. The Unity Conference is a powerful addition to an already dynamic community. As we know, it takes a combined effort from all involved to make America, and the state of Georgia, a place that we are proud to call home.

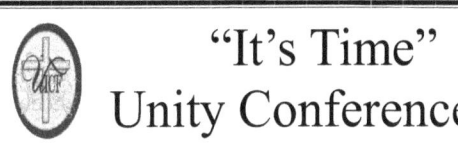

"It's Time"
Unity Conference

I Am A Business Woman

The mission and goal of UICF is to motivate and elevate. With that in mind, we established the "Learning with Love" program which encourages individually based GED preparation and subject matter tutoring.

The program grew out of a love for helping individuals become more academically fulfilled and enriched. One way was by accomplishing the goal of furthering their education.

If you were given an opportunity to have your own business, would you seize the moment?

If not, ask yourself why.

I Am A Business Woman

I Am ... His~

Inspirations from you~

Look up; move forward~

Inspirations from you~

I Am ... His~

I am a Child of God.

Jesus Christ almighty is my source of strength.

He has equipped me with the Holy Bible to lead and guide my life.

Fiery darts are struck down by my shield of faith.

I have been sheltered by the storm, showered with God's blessing, seized by His mercy, stripped of my iniquities, and saved by His grace.

I will honor my Father's will, I will not compromise, be put aside, be beat down, be tossed around, or be shut down.

I will be loving, kind, respectable, patient, and watchful.

Whatever my God asks me to do, I will do.

No assignment is too hard when asked by my God. Because, I am a Child of God.

My assurance is in knowing that whatever I need, He will supply.

Whether it is leading the choir, singing a song, facilitating a retreat, or just saying Amen.

He can count on me, because I am a Child of God.

He sits high and He looks low.

I am proud to be who I am.

I do not need to be called on, waited on, turned on, loved on, dependent on, lied on, or hit on.

I am grounded, resourceful, doing His will, searching my heart, praising the Lord, and preaching His word!

It's not necessary to feel sorry for me, fix food for me, have discussions about me, or pick up the pieces from my misery.

Neither do I need to be molded, modeled, mimicked, or manipulated.

I am strong.

Things that bother some folks, don't bother me at all.

You can't make me mad enough to give up on God.

Even when I'm tired I'll find time to do His will, for He is God all by Himself.

When God first called me, I was a babe; birthed by my mother and instructed by my father.

I Am ... His~

I Am A Child of God

I can't lose if God is my focus, I can't lose if God is my shield, and I can't lose if I trust in His Word.

You see, I can do all things through Christ who strengthens me.

This world can't deny me, burdens can't weaken me, opposition cannot harden me, and success cannot own me. Because, because, I am a Child of God.

You know what? The enemy can not stand me and what is even better is that I can not stand him either.

For one day my Father is going to call and I want to be ready.

I'm not going to let anyone turn me around; I will look up and move forward; I will walk and not get weary; and when I am finished down here,

I want the Lord to say well done, my good and faithful servant. Because, because,
I am a Child of God.
Amen,
Amen,
Amen.

I Am ... His~

***D**o you know the Lord today?* Have you invited Him into your heart? Do you believe that He died for you and for me; was crucified, died and was buried? But then He rose, and He now sits in glory.

Do you know Him?

If not, then confess with your mouth and believe with your heart and you too will become a Child of God.

I Am A Child of God

Inspirations from you~

Look up; move forward~

Inspirations from you~

Look up; move forward~

Introduction Excerpts from My Congressional Announcement

It is with great humility that I stand before you this afternoon with the opportunity to introduce to many and reintroduce to others a great woman of integrity. America is a country built on the ideas of visionaries whose desires were to honor God and serve man; from President George Washington, Harriett Tubman, to Dr. Martin L. King and others, and with the passing of each generation, this "mantle" of servant-hood is embraced by men and women who heed their divine calling.

Vivian Childs is one such person. Vivian is a native Georgian who early in life embraced the American concepts of "Life, Liberty, and the Pursuit of Happiness" and fought for equality in rights with other young activists of the Civil Rights Era. Committed to the idea of a better America, she embraced the Republican Party's conservative values and has emerged as one of Georgia's premier grassroots advocates.

Just ask grassroots conservatives, Young Republicans, Black Conservatives, females, veterans, and others of their commitment.

I Am ... His~

As Eighth District Chairman, Vivian travelled miles each year, covering 24 counties and a host of cities, training, empowering, and electing candidates to office - from local councils, school boards, state legislative positions, congressional, and presidential races.

Ms Vivian, as we call her, took it to the "streets," she put "boots on the ground." Unyielding in her principles, she kept everyone focused and marched candidates towards victory. In her community, she is known as principal, teacher, and board member for a host of organizations. She is a wife, a mother, and a minister. Yes, Ms. Vivian is truly "all" that.

Proverbs 29:2 states, "When the godly are in authority, the people rejoice. But when the wicked are in power, they groan." Vivian is a woman who has decided to embrace her divine calling. She is willing to take on the "mantle' of creating a better, godly government.

At this hour, it is my great honor to present to you Ms. Vivian. Let's all stand and give a rousing applause for Ms. Vivian Childs.

Recited by Author, Dr. Camilla J. Moore

~I Am In The Political Arena~

Inspirations from you~

Look up; move forward~

Inspirations from you~

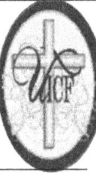

Sermon Epilogue

I pray that you have enjoyed the beats of my heart through verse and words.

Let me say this to you. If you grasp learning to obey, then you learn to deal with other things that are to come in your life. Think about this, if you can't learn to obey your parents, then you probably won't learn to obey God. Proverbs 1:15 says "My son, do not walk in the way with them.

Do not is a command. This sounds to me like a parent trying to stop a child from stepping into something; or better yet, a spouse hmmmm, maybe I will not go there.

I first titled this sermon, "God Favors Me," because He Does. Then it became, "Blessed and Highly Favored," because I believe I am. Then after spending a glorious Saturday with my church family, it became "Well Done." The sermon would also include many of my favorite songs.

Have you heard the phrase, *blessed and highly favored?* What does that saying mean to you. How many of you believe that you are? How many of you believe that every *Good Gift* and every Perfect Gift comes from above? How many of you like things to be Well Done?

I thought how that really gets to the meat of it. *Well Done*. I, for one, like things to be done well; especially, when I have been given a task. When you are asked to do something, give it your all, your best, do it well. When I thought about it, one of my favorite things to say is "when I meet my Savior face to face and I'm just standing there, like a child waiting for a piece of candy, I want to hear the Lord say two words, *"WELL Done!"*

At the cookout, as I stood over the grill, I said to someone that I like my food well done. Then I thought, I like more than food well done. I like things in general well done. We often say done well, but henceforth, I will say *well done*. It's something about putting *well* first that makes things better.

Think about it. Well-loved means you are loved better. For instance, when a teacher comments that Johnny is well-behaved, it means that Johnny's behavior is better than others. So, you see where I'm going with this.

On that day when the Lord says to us *well done*, He is telling us that we did it better than some others. So when you go to the restaurant the next time and order that juicy steak remember to order it how? *Well done.* Why? Because it's done better.

Think about this. People who are poisoned from uncooked food sometimes get sick, but when you get it *well done* you cook the germs away. JUST SAYING.

Let me tell you about my husband. *Sorry dear.* When we were dating, everything he ordered was medium. When we became engaged, sometimes medium well (notice, things are getting what, better). We married and after many, many years, he began to always order medium well after tasting what I had and noticing that it was better. Today, after 44 years, he finally has gotten it correct and wants his things *well done.*

Oh Yeah.!

My message is about each of us looking in the mirror and asking can we be better?

Are our souls well?

If you are without a church home, if the Lord is speaking to you, and if you think today is the day to say it is well in my soul; then right now,
ask Him into your heart.

Romans 10:9 says,"
That if thou shalt confess with thy mouth the Lord Jesus, and shalt believe in thine heart that God hath raised him from the dead, thou shalt be saved."

If you have prayed this prayer, I welcome you into this great gathering of family.
Amen~

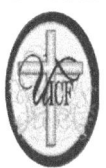

I Am ... His~

Inspirations from you~

Look up; move forward~

Inspirations from you~

Inspirations from you~

Look up; move forward~

Inspirations from you~

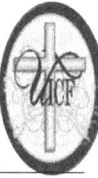

Coming Soon!

Raising Doctors
by Vivian L. Childs

Please feel free to contact us if you would like information on any of our products and services, or would like to request a speaker for your next engagement. We would love to hear from you.

VLCHILDS/UICF, LLC
PO Box 9334
Warner Robins, GA 31095

email: vlccreations@yahoo.com

Additionally, if you would like to join to help further the works of UICF (United In Christ Forever), please use the contact information listed above. Remember, we can do all things through Christ who strengthens us.

www.vivianchilds.com

Acknowledgements

Thank you once again for those who have accompanied me on this journey. I am who I am, because you are who you are:

a Christian, a mother, a dad, a husband, a friend, a minister, a wife, a son, a daughter, a sister, a teacher, a Gran-Gran, a poet, a principal, a volunteer, a politician, a Papa, a **singer**, a First Lady, a Pastor, a believer, an American, and *most importantly,* **HIS**

Be Blessed~

I Am ... His~

Other Books
By: Vivian Childs

The Day Before Christmas

By:
*Vivian L. Childs &
Mack W. Curry III*

I Am ... His~

In His Hand

By: Minister Vivian L. Childs

I Am ... His~

SPLINTERED

BROKENNESS IN THE

POLITICAL

ARENA

Are We Sacrificing America for Political Gain?

VIVIAN L. CHILDS

I Am ... His~

Sky Phoenix

Written and Illustrated by: Alexis Samara Childs

The Grand Bombaray

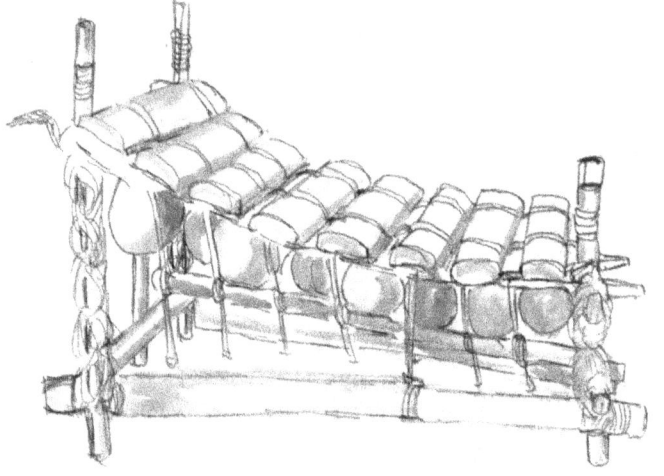

By: Nakeisha M. Curry, M.D

Illustrated by: Peggy Vesely

What or who do you see when you look in the mirror?

Who or what do you want to see when you look in the mirror?

Yes, you are all that!
Worthy, Caring, Loving

I Am ... His~

Tell yourself why~

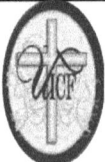

Inspirations from you~

Journal

Look up; move forward~

Inspirations from you~

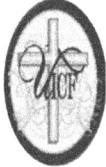

Pages

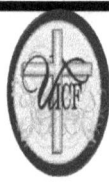
Inspirations from you~

Look up; move forward~

Inspirations from you~

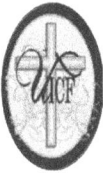

Look up; move forward~

Inspirations from you~

Look up; move forward~

Inspirations from you~

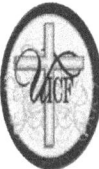

I Am ... His~

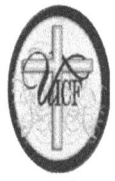
Inspirations from you~

152 *Look up; move forward~*

I Am ... His~

Inspirations from you~

Look up; move forward~

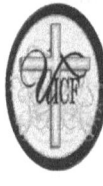

Inspirations from you~

Inspirations from you~

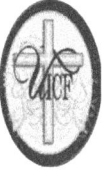

Look up; move forward~

What haven't you done that you would like to do?

What can you do to make it happen?

Write a note to a "Special Relative~"

I Am ... His~

Write a note to a "Special Friend~"

Inspirations from you~

Look up; move forward~

Inspirations from you~

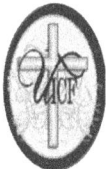

Look up; move forward~

I Am ... His~

Inspirations from you~

Look up; move forward~

Inspirations from you~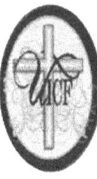

Look up; move forward~

Inspirations from you~

Look up; move forward~

Inspirations from you~

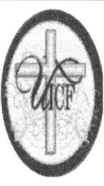

Look up; move forward~

I Am ... His~

Inspirations from you~

Look up; move forward~

Inspirations from you~

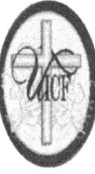

Look up; move forward~

Inspirations from you~

Look up; move forward~

Inspirations from you~

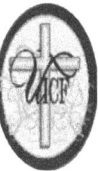

Look up; move forward~

I Am ... His~

Inspirations from you~

Look up; move forward~

Inspirations from you~

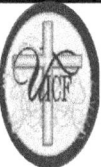

Inspirations from you~

Inspirations from you~

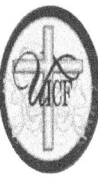

Look up; move forward~

Inspirations from you~

Look up; move forward~

I Am ... His~

Inspirations from you~

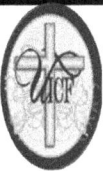

Look up; move forward~

I Am ... His~

Inspirations from you~

Look up; move forward~

Inspirations from you~

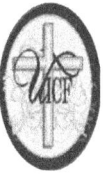

Inspirations from you~

Look up; move forward~

I Am ... His~

Inspirations from you~

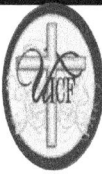

Look up; move forward~

Inspirations from you~

Look up; move forward~

I Am ... His~

Inspirations from you~

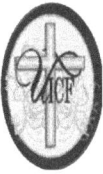

Look up; move forward~

I Am ... His~

Inspirations from you~

Look up; move forward~

Inspirations from you~

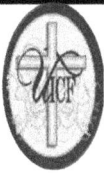

Look up; move forward~

Inspirations from you~

Look up; move forward~

Inspirations from you~

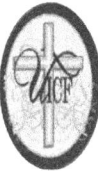

Look up; move forward~

I Am ... His~

Inspirations from you~

Look up; move forward~

Inspirations from you~

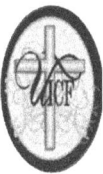

Look up; move forward~

I Am ... His~

Inspirations from you~

Look up; move forward~

Inspirations from you~

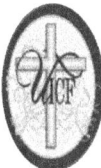

Inspirations from you~

Inspirations from you~

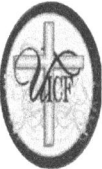

Inspirations from you~

Look up; move forward~

Inspirations from you~

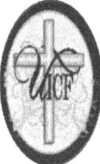

I Am ... His~

Inspirations from you~

Look up; move forward~

Inspirations from you~

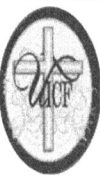

Look up; move forward~

Inspirations from you~

Look up; move forward~

Inspirations from you~

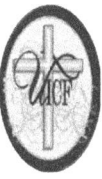

Look up; move forward~

Inspirations from you~

Look up; move forward~

I Am ... His~

Inspirations from you~

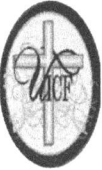

Look up; move forward~

I Am ... His~

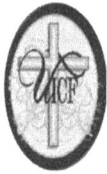

Inspirations from you~

Look up; move forward~

Inspirations from you~

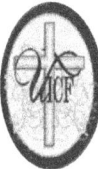

Look up; move forward~

I Am ... His~

Inspirations from you~

Look up; move forward~

Inspirations from you~

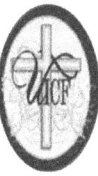

Look up; move forward~

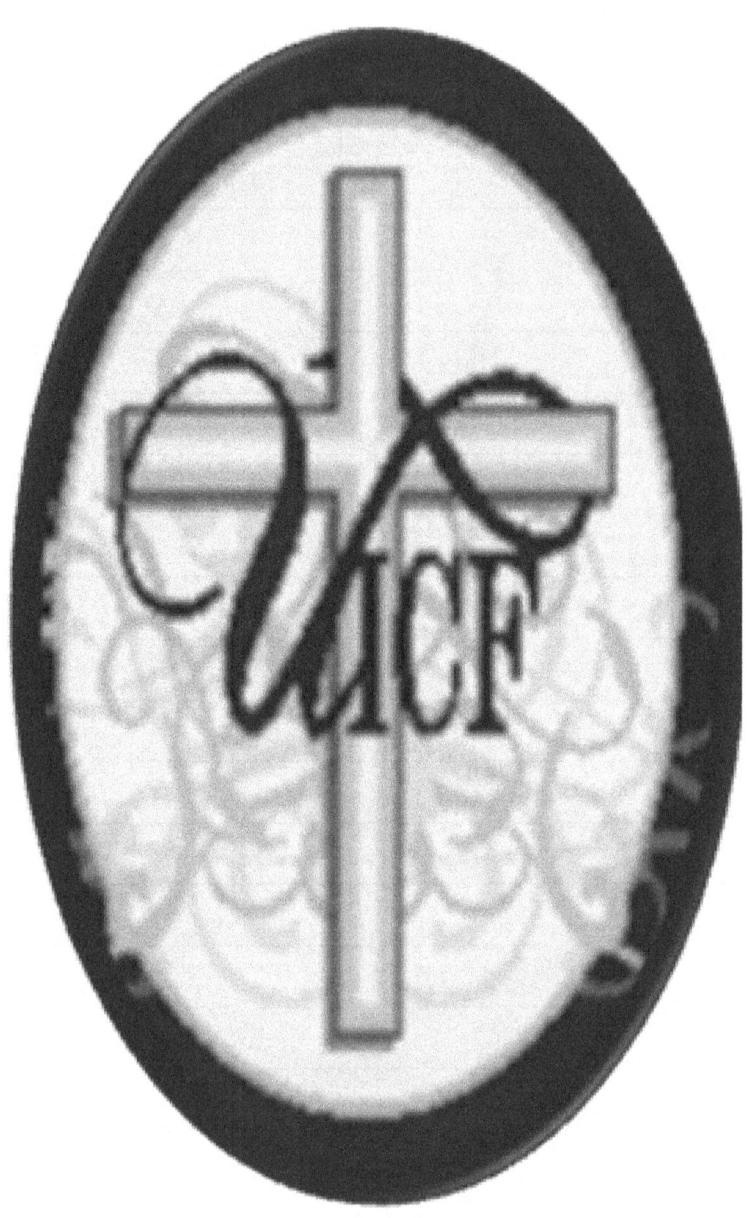

www.ingramcontent.com/pod-product-compliance
Lightning Source LLC
Chambersburg PA
CBHW071706090426
42738CB00009B/1677